The Vision Journal

A whole brain journal and portable vision board

The Vision Journal
Sara Marchessault

Published by Joyful by Design in 2020
Second edition; First printing

Copyright © 2020 Joyful by Design, LLC

joyfulbydesign.com

Cover background image from Sara Marchessault

All Rights Reserved. Do not share or forward this work, or reproduce any portion by any means, without written permission of the author. Fair use of quotes and key concepts must be appropriately cited.

Sara Marchessault is a journaling expert who creates and develops products and services to teach and support the use of self-reflection for a more fulfilling and productive life.

Learn more at www.saramarchessault.com.

Find Sara Marchessault on:
Facebook
Twitter
Pinterest

ISBN 978-1-7340288-1-2

For Faith

*"Create the highest,
grandest vision possible
for your life,
because you become
what you believe."
– Oprah Winfrey*

You are in the right place.

Sanctuary may be found in these pages.

In the midst of sanctuary comes peace. Understanding. Room to breathe.

And creation.

Creation of something new and breathtaking.

Big and sweeping. Or maybe small and tender.

Something that starts with the glimmer of an idea in the pit of your stomach. Or behind your eyes, in the cave where your deepest desires and dreams live and seek refuge, waiting for the day you turn the light inward, bringing them out into the open to move from ideas to experiences lived.

In the pages of this journal, you are invited to explore the depths of those caves. See what you find there and follow your instinct as to if and when to bring your findings into the light.

The Vision Journal is a whole-brain approach to journaling. Bear with me while this gets a little geeky for a minute. Each of us has a unique way that we think. And when our brain is firing neurons in the pattern that is uniquely ours, we may be thinking in words or images. Or some of each.

The Vision Journal has been designed for you to engage both of these sensibilities. There is space in the pages here for you to express your wants, desires, deepest thoughts, dreams, and what-ifs in the words that ring true for you.

This sanctuary is the place for you to let out what you need to get out. Swear. Use a Sharpie. Write in teeny tiny letters that only a fairy could read. Don't hold back.

Describe the perfect job, the dream house, the spouse who sweeps you off your feet. Consider solutions. Solve problems. The process of writing will peel away the curtains of uncertainty to reveal the brightness of new insight.

Your sanctuary in this journal also has space for you to add your own images. When we work with both images and words, we engage the entire brain in our intentions. When this happens, what we want and desire become a part of us. And we are much more likely to create the experience when we are fully vested in having it.

You will see the difference here between space for words on lined pages and space for images on colored pages. Remember though, this is your journal, your sanctuary. There are no rules here. Write where it feels good to write and put images where you feel they need to be.

Fair warning: As you use this journal to create the experiences of your life in both words and images, strange things may start to happen.

Resources will become available that you didn't know you had. You may get an email inviting you to apply to a grant for money to start your own business. You will meet a person on a plane who teaches guitar to adults in small groups via online classes. You may be out driving and see a sign for a farmer's market you didn't know was there, explore, and find a new place to buy local, organic eggs.

Resources are opportunities that you choose to use or not. When we engage with a resource, we are using an opportunity to create something spectacular. When Aunt Sally's best friends husbands sister-in-law offers you to come in for an interview for a job in your dream industry, this is an opportunity for you to use your resources.

When we start working with both images and words to create the vision for our life, the support we need to live the experience we desire makes its way to us.

We have to be open to see the resources as gifts and express gratitude for them. We have to be brave to take the opportunities that require bold action to live the life we want.

Are you ready?

Is it time for you to engage yourself fully in the life you wish for and desire?

If you're here, that's a pretty good sign the answer is yes.

When you wake up in the morning, you are living a life that you create. If you want that life to be different, the first step is to have a vision for what you want.

So go ahead. Swing by the store and pick up a new pen that gets you excited to write. Pull out your stack of old magazines from the garage and start to flip through looking for images that resonate with you.

Spend time in your sanctuary and pay attention to what you learn about yourself while you're in there. See what ideas expand in your mind to become possibilities.

And then watch possibilities become realities.

Love,
Sara

Using Your New Journal

The first how-to for this journal is that there is no how-to for this journal. This is your space to do with what you will. Write, color, tear, paste, insert, store; The Vision Journal is your oyster!

There are two types of pages in this book, simply because there are clear advantages to both lined and unlined pages.

Lined pages keep words neat and orderly, making it easier to go back and reread them. Unlined pages allow for more freedom with your writing utensil. You can write in circles, draw, and allow yourself to explore a little more.

Lines can make a journaler feel restricted; blank pages can release your wild side!

Lines can also provide the structure that we all crave at one point or another. Unlined pages are great for inserting photos or images from magazines that resonate with you.

How you use the pages is up to you. This is your sanctuary.

Prompting questions in your journal.

Several questions have been listed at the front end of The Vision Journal to help jumpstart the wheels in your brain. You can use these any way you like.

Work your way through the list of questions and answer each one as you move through your journal.

Find the questions you like and respond to them as you see fit.

Choose one question that resonates with you and answer it each day for a week in your journal to see if your response changes and if you learn something new about yourself.

Or, don't use the questions at all.

Pay attention to what you need in any given moment. Don't respond to a question because you think you have to. Use the prompt because you want to. Because writing an answer to that particular question gets you pumped to move your pen across the page.

Prompting Questions

Think of these as brainstorming prompts, a place to start thinking about who you are and what is most important to you.

- Am I currently living a life filled with meaning? Am I the person I want to be?
  - What does it mean to me to live a life with meaning?
  - How can I measure whether or not I am the person I want to be?
  - Do I hop out of bed in the morning, ready to take on the world and happy with my life? (Do I even want to be an out-of-bed hopper?)

- What would you do if failing didn't matter?
  - What are you so excited about learning/experiencing/trying that if you are no good at all, it totally does not matter?

- Describe a time that you were deeply, truly happy.
  - Close your eyes and think back to a time when you felt whole, complete, and satisfied. All is right with the world in this moment and you are filled with a sense of calm and knowing.

- How do you want to be remembered?
  - Imagine a celebration of your life and accomplishments. Who do you want to see there and what do you want them to say about you?
  - Do the actions and choices you make today support what you want to hear at this celebration?

- Determine your roles and relationship priorities.
  - Make a list of the roles you play in your life (mother, student, wife, business owner, employee, etc.). Include those you currently play often and those you'd like to play.
  - Review your list and check each role where you've invested more than five hours in the last thirty days.
  - How many roles had no checkmark? How does this reflect the life you want to live and the life you are actually living?
  - Circle the most important role without a checkmark. Write about yourself in that role. What are you doing? How are you different? Are you living the life you want as you grow in this role? Let your vision be expressed on the page.
  - If desired, assign your roles a ranking or letter grade and evaluate where you are in each role. What will you have to change in order to make your vision for each role become a reality?

- Instead of focusing on the question of how, e.g. "how am I going to do this," try focusing on the what.
  - What is the first step?
  - What will I do next?

- What is holding you back right now in your life? Take a good look around and think about what is keeping you from living your vision.
  - Explore how your roadblocks add or change your vision. If you could remove them, what wonderful things would occur?

- What is the game in life that you really want to be playing?
  - Be bold and name the game! Describe the players you want to join your team and define what it means to succeed at your game.

- What about your life excites you? What upsets you?

- Where do you see yourself in five years? Ten years? How will the actions you take today contribute to making that vision a reality?

- What does your vision smell like? What does it taste like?

- Is your vision compelling you to take action?
  - Do you have a dream that you take strides to make real or does it sit on a shelf and linger, a whisper in the back of your mind? How committed are you to making this dream more than an idea and into something tangible?

- What can you do to make sure your vision is part of your daily practice?
  - Does thinking about your vision give you joy? If so, think of a way to bring it into your presence more often. Write a sentence on an index card and keep it in your pocket. Carry The Vision Journal with you and open it at least once a day to write, add images, or review your entries.

- List 10 things you are thankful for. What does it feel like to be thankful? How does gratitude play into your vision?

- Consider creating a board of people to provide you with feedback and support. Share your vision with them and talk regularly about your current actions as they compare to achieving your vision. If it feels right for you, document their feedback in The Vision Journal.
  - And of course, do the same for them!

- Do you have a goal in mind you'd like to accomplish? Write a letter to a friend or loved one from the perspective of having accomplished that goal.
  - Include lots of detail on how it felt to experience this achievement, the work you did to make it happen, the challenges along the way, etc. Don't forget to express your gratitude for the support of others!

- What images feel right to put on this page?
  - Grab a stack of old magazines or photos. Take a deep breath and open yourself up to the experience of simply sorting through images, trusting that the ones you need will make themselves known to you.

Journaling is meditative: breathe, move the pen, and let the goodness from your soul ooze into your mind and heart.

Ritual

"No matter what happens, or how bad it seems today,
life does go on, and it will be better tomorrow."
- Maya Angelou

Courage

Be Open

"Dare to be brave today and then when you extend your wings, you will fly."

– Mary DeMuth

Clarity

"Write it on your heart that every day is the
best day in the year."
- Ralph Waldo Emerson

Trust

What do you treasure?

"The desire to reach for the stars is ambitious. The desire to reach hearts is wise."

- Maya Angelou

Bold

"Never laugh at live dragons."
- J. R. R. Tolkein

Serenity

Explore

"When nothing is sure, everything is possible."

– Margaret Drabble

"Each day comes bearing its own gifts.
Untie the ribbons."
- Rumi

Thrive

"There are times when life surprises one, and
anything may happen, even what one had hoped for."
- Ellen Glasgow

Go for Gutsy

"One should always act from one's inner sense of rhythm."

– Rosamond Lehmann

Now

"There is no life that does not contribute to history."
- Dorothy West

Renew

What did you nourish today?

"Mistakes are part of the dues one pays for a full life."

– Sophia Loren

"Love the moment and the energy of that moment
will spread beyond all boundaries."
- Cortia Kent

Flexible

"Sometimes opportunity knocks, but most of the time
it sneaks up and then quietly steals away."
- Doug Larson

Uplifted

"If you have built castles in the air, your work need not be lost. That is where they should be. Now put foundations under them."

– Henry David Thoreau

Allow

"I am not pretty. I am not beautiful.
I am as radiant as the sun."
- Suzanne Collins

Attention

Shine

"The self is not something ready made, but something in continuous formation through choice of action."

– John Dewey

"Don't spend time beating on a wall, hoping to
transform it into a door."
- Coco Chanel

Risk

"Happiness is a warm puppy."
- Charles M. Schulz

Flourish

"Any road is bound to arrive somewhere if you follow it far enough."

– Patricia Wentworth

Laughter

"The greatest thing about dreams is they don't expire. They can lay dormant for years and when you pull them out and dust them off, they shine like new."
- Casi McLean

Fulfilled

Dearest Fellow Journaler,

Before we talk about what comes next, can I just say, well done, friend.

Not many people take the time to dive into their dreams. To allow themselves to really think about what they want. To play with visions and words just for the pleasure of doing so.

To dream about what is possible.

So, what comes next?

In here you have ideas and desires. You have to ask yourself if they will remain ideas and desires, living only in your imagination, or if you want to call these ideas and desires into your reality.

There is one sure sign that you have reached a time where you want to make changes happen in your life. To take the ideas from the pages and work to bring them into your everyday experience.

Restlessness.

A yearning to make something be different. Longing for adventure. Dissatisfaction with your work in the world. A craving for more meaningful relationships.

A need to look in the mirror and see a different look on your face.

You might feel testy. Cranky. Uncomfortable in your own skin.

You might find that you're telling yourself that everything is all right when it really isn't.

Restless.

I want you to know that it's perfectly all right. This feeling is the precursor to making change. When you feel it, you need only ask yourself if you are ready. And if you are, then take the plunge.

That doesn't mean you have to run wild, quit your job right away, leave your husband, and head to Nebraska to grow corn with a Latin Lover.

Although if that is what your soul really wants…obviously go for it.

Usually restlessness can be addressed by making one change. Apply for one new job a week. Try a new exercise routine you've been wondering about for the last year. Buy a set of paints and open them up.

Listen to the voice that's telling you that you want to change and take one step.

And if you're really into making waves, support and accountability will work wonders in moving you forward as you work to make change.

It all starts here. It started the minute you picked up this journal and decided to explore the most meaningful roadmap you will ever possess – your own desires.

Here's to your joyful journaling and making your life happen!
Love,
Sara

www.ingramcontent.com/pod-product-compliance
Lightning Source LLC
Chambersburg PA
CBHW081358070526
44583CB00020B/2590